A GUIDE TO Little House COUNTRY

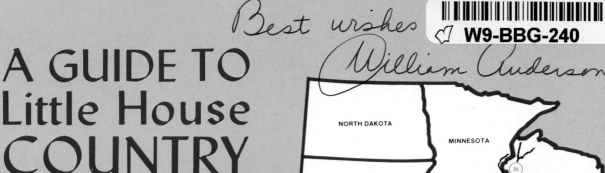

PEPIN, WISCONSIN

In town is a Laura Ingalls Wilder Park, and a museum. Seven miles northwest is the "Little House Wayside" with a cabin restoration of Laura's 1867 birthplace.
Write: Laura Ingalls Wilder
Memorial Society
Box 269
Pepin, WI 54759

INDEPENDENCE, KANSAS

Thirteen miles from town is the replica of the Ingalls cabin on the present-day William Kurtis ranch.
Write: Little House on the Prairie
Box 110
Independence, KS 67301

WALNUT GROVE, MINNESOTA

In town is the Wilder Museum and two miles north is the Ingalls homesite and dugout remains along Plum Creek. The Ingalls-based pageant "Fragments of a Dream" is performed open-air in the month of July.
Write: Laura Ingalls Wilder Museum
Box 58
Walnut Grove, MN 56180

BURR OAK, IOWA

Not featured in the "Little House" series, but home of the Ingalls in 1876-1877. The restored Masters Hotel, where the family lived, is open to the public.
Write: Laura Ingalls Wilder
Park and Museum
Box 354
Burr Oak, IA 52131

DE SMET, SOUTH DAKOTA

Home of Laura, 1879-1894; final stopping place for her family. Visitors can see 17 sites mentioned in the books, including the Ingalls Home and Surveyors' House.
Write: Laura Ingalls Wilder
Memorial Society
Box 344
De Smet, SD 57231

MANSFIELD, MISSOURI

Rocky Ridge Farm was the home of Laura, Almanzo and Rose Wilder. The house and museum next to it contains almost everything the Wilders owned and used. In town is the Wilder Library and the graves of the family.
Write: Laura Ingalls Wilder Home-Museum
Rt. 1, Box 24
Mansfield, MO 65704

MALONE, NEW YORK

The home of "Farmer Boy" on a farm 3½ miles from town is currently in the process of restoration.
Write: Almanzo and Laura Ingalls Wilder
Association
Box 283
Malone, NY 12953

INGALLS FAMILY-1890's

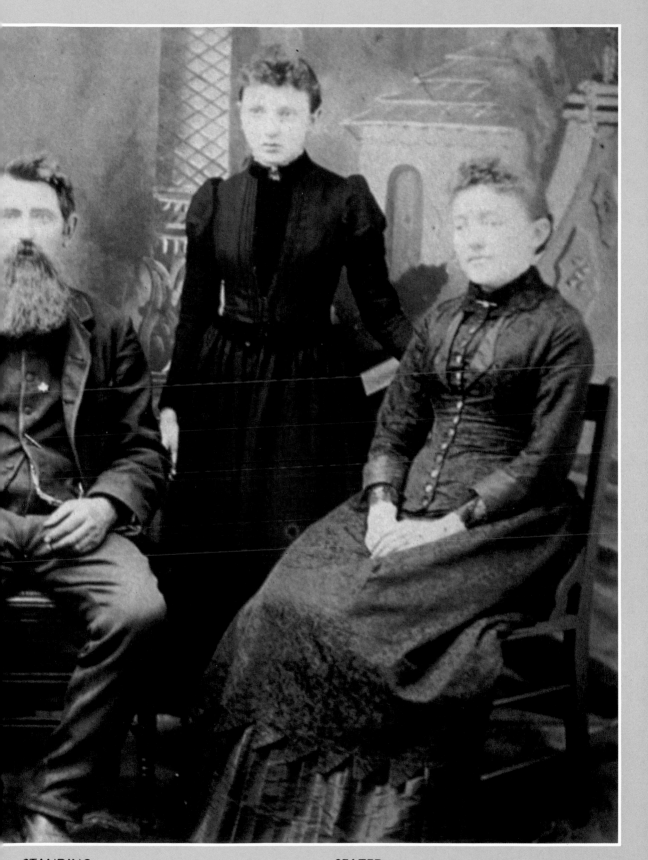

STANDING
CARRIE (SWANZEY) 1870-1946
LAURA (WILDER) 1867-1957
GRACE (DOW) 1877-1941

SEATED
CAROLINE QUINER INGALLS (MA) 1839-1924
CHARLES PHILIP INGALLS (PA) 1836-1902
MARY 1865-1928

Pepin, Wisconsin's Laura Ingalls Wilder Memorial Society was formed to commemorate a great Wisconsin author. In 1978, a reconstructed replica of the Ingalls' cabin was dedicated, the original having vanished years before. The wayside is just off Highway 183, seven miles from the village of Pepin.

Charles and Caroline Ingalls bought their land in the "Big Woods" in 1863, three years after their marriage. Here their first two children, Mary and Laura, were born in 1865 and 1867. When Laura started her writing career as a children's author at the age of 65 in 1932, she recalled in *Little House in the Big Woods* the warm firelit cabin, the tall trees and the forests full of wild animals. "Now is now. It can never be a long time ago," she wrote as she ended her first book. Through her writing and this restored site, "a long time ago" lives again.

FAMILY RECORD.

MARRIAGES

Married in Concord Jefferson Co. Wisconsin, by Rev. J. W. Lyman, Charles P. Ingalls to Caroline C. Quiner, Feb. 1st 1860,

FAMILY RECORD.

BIRTHS.

Mary Amelia Ingalls born Tuesday Jan. 10 1865. Town Pepin Pepin Co. Wisconsin.

Laura Elizabeth Ingalls born Thursday Feb. 8th 1867 Town of Pepin Pepin Co Wisconsin

Caroline Celestia Ingalls born Wednesday Aug 3, 1870. Montgomery Co. Kansas.

Charles Frederic Ingalls Born monday Nov. 1st 1875 Town North Hero Redwood Co Minnesota.

Grace Pearl Ingalls Co Tuesday May 23d 1877 in the Town of Burr Oak Winneshiek Co Iowa

The Ingalls Family Bible (above) was acquired by Pa and Ma after their marriage and was mentioned in *Little House in the Big Woods*. Ma's fine handwriting records the birth of the children. The Bible is now on display at the Laura Ingalls Wilder Home and Museum in Mansfield, Missouri.

A Wisconsin historic marker explains the history of the Ingalls family on this land. Another marker memorializes Laura Ingalls Wilder in the town park in Pepin.

LITTLE HOUSE WAYSIDE

"Once upon a time......a little girl lived in the Big Woods of Wisconsin in a little gray house made of logs."

Writing about herself and her life here, Laura Ingalls Wilder thus began "Little House in the Big Woods," the first of her famous "Little House" books.

Laura was born here on February 7, 1867. Late in 1868 or in the spring of 1869, the Ingalls family left Wisconsin and traveled by covered wagon to Kansas. They found Kansas to be Indian country, so shortly after Carrie was born in August of 1870, Charles Ingalls brought his family back to the little house near Pepin. In 1871 Mary and Laura enrolled in the Barry Corner School near here. They sold this farm in 1873 and moved to Minnesota.

Laura Ingalls Wilder is loved, both for her delightful writing style and for her good homespun philosophy. Reflecting on her rugged frontier youth, she said "It has been many years since I beat eggs with a fork or cleaned a kerosene lamp. Many things have changed since then, but the truths we learned from our parents and the principles they taught us are always true. They can never change."

The Laura Ingalls Wilder Memorial Society, Inc. of Pepin, Wisconsin, organized in 1974, is proud to provide "Little House Wayside" as a memorial to this great lady and beloved author.

Erected 1978

Laura Ingalls Wilder was awe-struck when she first saw Lake Pepin, a spot which Mark Twain called one of the most beautiful places in the world. The lake, actually a widened extent of the Mississippi River, is part of "The Great River Road." When the Ingalls family left the area for points west, they crossed the lake on the frozen ice and climbed the bluffs on the Minnesota side. Laura revisited the area with her husband Almanzo in 1890.

The village of Pepin (*below*) includes antique shops, the Pepin Depot Museum, the Wilder Park and opportunities for fishing, swimming and sailing. Scenic overlooks abound in and around this old river town.

LITTLE HOUSE
ON THE PRAIRIE
NEXT RIGHT

Owners of the property, Bill and Wilma Kurtis, have cooperated totally in making the site of *Little House on the Prairie* near Independence, Kansas available for visitors. The cabin replica was rebuilt after painstaking research by Margaret Clement of Independence, who pinpointed the site.

Near the cabin is the original well (*below*) which Pa dug in *Little House on the Prairie*. Oil and gas is pumped from the former Ingalls' land, explaining the gassy fumes encountered during the well digging described by Laura.

Prairie life was an adventure for Laura Ingalls. The grasses were alive with insects, rabbits and flowers.

Near the Ingalls' cabin replica is a one-room school taught in 1901 by the mother of Wilma Kurtis, and the historic former post office from Wayside, Kansas.

This is the creek (above) which Mr. Edwards crossed to bring Christmas presents for the Ingalls girls.

Dr. George Tann, the well-known black physician to the Indians and pioneers, was mentioned in *Little House on the Prairie*. He is buried in Independence, Kansas.

At the *Little House on the Prairie* site, visitors can relive a pioneer school experience. "I went to little red schoolhouses all over the west," Laura recalled.

Buffalo roam near the "Little House" site today.

When the Ingalls family moved to Plum Creek, near Walnut Grove, Minnesota in 1873, they first lived in a dugout. The site is now marked.

The present day footbridge over Plum Creek leads visitors to the dugout site.

Table Rock

Wild plums still thrive near the dugout site.

"On the Banks of Plum Creek."

Visitors to Walnut Grove can see historic exhibits and artifacts at the museum in town.

Laura Ingalls
FREE MUSE
INFORMATION
WALNUT GRO

On exhibit in the Walnut Grove Museum is an original Ingalls quilt.

Wilder
M AND
ENTER
, MN.

The original church bell from the Congregational Church is the one Pa helped pay for. It now rings in the English Lutheran Church of Walnut Grove.

Laura said: "With my parents and sisters, I traveled in a prairie schooner."

Not mentioned in her "Little House" books was the time Laura's family lived in the village of Burr Oak, Iowa. Pa and Ma helped to operate the Masters Hotel, and the family lived there late in 1876. The hotel is now restored for visitors to see.

"Our hotel was built on a side hill. A door from the main street opened into the bar-room, then across the hall was the parlor, also with a street door."
—Laura Ingalls Wilder

"Across the street we looked into a terraced lawn of a big white house. Mr. Piper, who owned the big house, was very rich and the house was very beautiful."

"The graveyard was a beautiful place...The white stones standing amid all this beauty didn't look lonesome."

"Going after the cow was the happiest time of the day. The oak woods were always a joy."

—Laura Ingalls Wilder

The Masters Hotel (*left*) as it appeared in an earlier day.

"Never a break to mar their sweep of grandeur
From North to South, from East to West the same,
Save that the East was full of purple shadows,
The West with setting sun was all aflame."
from "*The Dakota Prairies*"
by Laura Ingalls Wilder

Site of Silver Lake, near De Smet, South Dakota.

In 1879, Charles and Caroline Ingalls moved their family from Walnut Grove, Minnesota to the site of De Smet, South Dakota (then Dakota Territory). This is the site of the Ingalls homestead claim, which was a setting in the books *By the Shores of Silver Lake*, *The Long Winter*, *Little Town on the Prairie*, and *These Happy Golden Years*.

After Laura's wedding in 1885, she and her husband Almanzo Wilder farmed this tree claim north of De Smet.

WILDER HOMESTEAD AND BIRTHPLACE OF ROSE WILDER LANE

On the low hill immediately west of this spot stood the homestead claim shanty of Almanzo and Laura Ingalls Wilder. Mrs. Wilder (1867-1957) is known all over the world as the author of the "Little House" books, a series of autobiographical accounts of pioneering by the Ingalls and Wilder families. Six of her books have their settings in the De Smet area. *The First Four Years* tells of farm life at this location from 1885-1889.

A shanty on the hilltop was the birthplace of the Wilders' only surviving child Rose Wilder Lane (1886-1968). Mrs. Lane became a well-known novelist, journalist and political essayist. Two of her 1930's novels, *Free Land* and *Let The Hurricane Roar* describe South Dakota pioneering. She also wrote biographies, translated books and served as a foreign correspondent. Her last reporting assignment took her to Viet Nam in 1965, when at 78 Rose Wilder Lane was America's oldest war correspondent. Although her career included travels around the world, Mrs. Lane stated that the entire pattern of her life was formed by the immense prairie skies, the acres of waving grain and the struggling saplings of her Dakota childhood.

One and one half miles north of this spot is another quarter section of land which was the tree claim of Laura and Almanzo Wilder. Some of the original tree plantings still survive. Here the Wilders also lived during their early married life, experiencing a fire which destroyed their home, the death of an infant son and other natural disasters which were a part of the daily lives of the courageous South Dakota pioneers. "No one," Mrs. Wilder wrote, "who has not pioneered can understand the fascination and the terror of it."

On the Wilder's homestead, their only surviving child, Rose, was born on December 5, 1886. William Anderson's text on this marker *(at left)* explains Rose's life and career and the history of this land.

The Surveyors' House (left) was the first home of the Ingalls family through the winter of 1879-1880.

The last home of the Ingalls (below) was built by Pa in 1887, on Third Street in De Smet. Pa and Ma lived out their lives here. The house was restored in 1972.

"In June when the prairie roses bloomed we would stop and gather them, filling the buggy with fragrant blossoms." Laura told her daughter Rose that "You are named for them, my dear."

The original building (below) of the First Congregational Church, where the Ingalls were charter members. Pa helped construct this church.

Laura and Carrie attended the first school in De Smet in this building.

The Surveyors' House originally stood on the north bank of Silver Lake, which was drained in the 1920's. It has been on its present location since the 1880's. The Laura Ingalls Wilder Memorial Society restored the house in 1967-1968.

"You'll never find a cozier home," Rose Wilder Lane said of the Ingalls home in De Smet. Laura never lived here, but she visited this house many times; in 1902 she came here when Pa died, and last visited the home in 1931.

A frosty winter sunrise over Silver Lake shows the bleak Dakota prairie in tones of gray and white.

Sunrise in deep winter silhouetting the stark bare branches of Pa's cottonwoods on the homestead claim is reminiscent of *The Hard Winter of 1880-1881*.

Winter at the tree claim of Laura and Almanzo, north of De Smet. Some of Almanzo's 1880's plantings still thrive.

The original Loftus store building (*above*) still stands on De Smet's historic main street (Calumet Avenue).

The dry lake bed of Silver Lake (*at right*), looking towards the Ingalls' homestead land.

The road at Lake Henry (*below*), where Laura and Almanzo rode in the buggy during courting days described in *These Happy Golden Years*.

Next to the Surveyors' House (*above*) is the headquarters of The Laura Ingalls Wilder Memorial Society. A tour of the Wilder sites begins here.

A visitor and tour guide (*left*) enjoy a memory of Laura in the gift shop.

A complete selection of Laura Ingalls Wilder books and souvenirs are available from The Society's gift shop in De Smet. Write for a price list.

"The Surveyors' House" is restored to its description in Laura's first South Dakota book, *By the Shores of Silver Lake*. The surveyors' stove was described by Laura as having two oven doors. So does this one.

A whatnot shelf (*right*) was built by the Ingalls the winter they spent in the Surveyors' House.

Pa, Ma and Grace used the downstairs bedroom (*center right*), while Laura and her sisters slept in the attic.

In the Surveyors' House the original organ (*left above*) from De Smet's first church is now displayed.

Hay twists (*above*) provided fuel during shortages described in Laura's book *The Long Winter*.

Ma's red-checked cloths (*at left*) made a cheerful spot in the house.

Pa Ingalls built this bureau (*below*). Laura tells of finding her hidden Christmas gift in a lower drawer in *Little Town on the Prairie*.

Laura was impressed with the well stocked Surveyors' Pantry (*at left*) for use during the winter of 1879-1880.

The lean-to (*below*) of the Surveyors' House is filled with old tools.

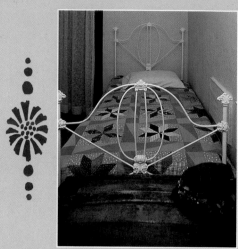

Blind Mary's bedroom (*above left*) was on the first floor of the house. She lived here with Pa and Ma after finishing the Iowa College for the Blind in 1889.

The dining room at the Pa and Ma Ingalls' home (*above*). Ma installed a wall telephone in 1916.

The built-in cupboards (*left*) in the Ingalls' kitchen were built by Pa.

Pa and Ma's bedroom (*below*), showing Ma's trunk and Rose Wilder Lane's wash stand. An original family quilt is on the bed.

Caroline Ingalls
Charles Ingalls

A view *(above)* of the Ingalls' parlor.

One of Carrie Ingalls' first snapshots with
her box camera *(right)* was this rare inte-
rior of the Ingalls' home parlor. Ma posed
with the portrait of Pa over her shoulder.
The "rope line" was a flaw which occured
while Carrie was developing this 1905
photograph.

The Parlor *(below)* in the Ingalls' home.
Grace was married here in 1901.

Some of Rose's furniture *(above)* sent to De Smet for display following her death in 1968.

One of Rose Wilder Lane's typewriters *(left)* used during her career as novelist, journalist, historian, and short fiction writer.

Rose's desk *(below left)* from her home in Danbury, Connecticut.

The narrow twisting stairway of the Ingalls' house *(below)*.

MOTHER
CAROLINE INGALLS
1839 — 1924

Ma's grave *(above)*. All the family are buried together in De Smet Cemetery, except Laura.

Ma selected this tombstone *(right)* for Pa when he died in 1902.

Mary learned to read both braille and raised print. *(Below)* This is one volume (of eight) of Mary's copy of *The Holy Bible*.

One of the three upstairs bedrooms *(below)* in the Ingalls' house.

VOLUME 6 OF THE OLD
TESTAMENT PRINTED IN
EMBOSSED (RAISED) PRINT

THIS BOOK BELONGED TO
MARY INGALLS

In 1941 Carrie left this
book in the care of Mrs.
John Rundell (Maude Noble)
in Manchester, South Dakota

Artifacts of the Ingalls family on display in De Smet includes Ma's shawl, a lap-desk, family photos, Grace's autograph book, Mary's beadwork and a glass box treasured by Carrie.

Famous "Little House" illustrator Garth Williams visited De Smet in 1986. He toured the sites and met hundreds of admirers.

This is the homestead site of
CHARLES AND CAROLINE INGALLS
and their daughters
Mary, Laura, Carrie and Grace

In four of her Little House series of stories of pioneering by the Ingalls and Wilder families, Laura Ingalls Wilder, beloved writer for children, has told of the Fall and Winter the family spent at a railway construction camp "By the Shores of Silver Lake" (1879-80) then moved to the townsite of De Smet, "Little Town on the Prairie" a mile west, to live in the Ingalls Store Building briefly, then move to a claim shanty on this site, across The Big Slough from the town. Here Pa planted the cottonwoods that still stand, and Ma made a home for her family. After the October Blizzard they returned to the town to spend "The Long Winter" (1880-81). One of the schools Laura was to teach was a mile south of this site. In "These Happy Golden Years" she told of her romance and marriage to Almanzo Wilder and their life in a claim shanty two miles north of De Smet, where their daughter, Rose Wilder Lane, journalist and author, was born. Mrs. Wilder died Feb. 11, 1957, aged 90, at the farm in the Ozarks near Mansfield, Mo., where they had lived since 1894.

DEDICATED JUNE 10, 1961
THIS PLOT DONATED BY EDWARD E. MAY, OWNER

Prairie boulder with marker text by Aubrey Sherwood, on the Ingalls' homestead.

"In Search of the Land of Milk and Honey"
Original Oil Painting by Harvey Dunn
On exhibit at Hazel Meyer Library, De Smet, South Dakota.

From the Aubrey Sherwood Collection

Harvey Dunn (1884-1952), a relative of the Ingalls family through marriage, became a renowned illustrator, teacher, and prairie painter. His returns to the De Smet area from his New Jersey studio led to a gift of several of his originals to the Hazel Meyer Library in De Smet, and the bulk of his art to South Dakota State University. They are on permanent exhibit in the Memorial Art Center at Brookings.

"Harvey Dunn has done a great thing in his paintings and it does seem as though they and my stories should be connected in some way. I should be proud to have our names connected because of our work."
—Laura Ingalls Wilder

ALMANZO WILDER
1857-1949
"The Man of the Place"

Laura (*above*), nicknamed "Bessie" by Almanzo and "Mama Bess" by daughter Rose.

The Wilders moved to Rocky Ridge Farm (*at left*) in Mansfield, Missouri from De Smet in 1894. The trip is described in *On the Way Home*. Together, Almanzo and Laura built up a farm and constructed their house.

"There is no other country in the world like the Ozarks", Laura wrote. The ten room Wilder home (above) was built from farm materials.

"My mother wished so much that the house could be kept as a memorial...someone had suggested it and she often spoke of it. She would be so happy to know that people want to do it. She was really very shy but she treasured every bit of affection that was shown her. Nothing would have pleased her more than knowing that Mansfield people want to keep her house in memory of her."
—Rose Wilder Lane

It was Rose Wilder Lane's initial generosity and cooperation that allowed for the preservation of her parents' home and their belongings for the enjoyment of "Little House" book readers.

Pa's Fiddle, given to Laura after her father's death, is now on display in the museum on Rocky Ridge. No one knows how Pa acquired it on the frontier.

The parlor (*above*) was the tenth and last room the Wilders added to the house in 1912. The rock fireplace was Laura's special request.

The cypress knee table was made by Almanzo from a Florida stump. It sits in an alcove of the parlor.

Almanzo arranged an alcove library (*above*) for Laura's books in a corner of the parlor.

A book given to Ma (Caroline Ingalls) (*above*) by her mother Charlotte Holbrook in 1860. Ma passed it on to Laura Ingalls Wilder.

The old pump organ (*left*) was a part of the Wilder home since the turn of the century. It is like the one Laura bought for Mary.

Original oil by W.H.D. Koerner (*right*) used on the cover of *The Saturday Evening Post* in 1932 to illustrate Rose Wilder Lane's "Let the Hurricane Roar".

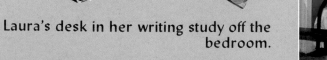

Laura's desk in her writing study off the bedroom.

Laura's books (*above*) were all written on 50/50 school tablets which she purchased for a nickel apiece. She wrote in pencil.

Laura and Almanzo's bedroom.

The dining room (*above*), showing Laura's favorite rocker. She once wrote an article on "The Farm Dining Room" for *The Country Gentleman* in 1925.

The porch (*below*) off the dining room was a favored place to eat and relax in the summers on Rocky Ridge Farm.

Laura's article "My Ozark Kitchen" in *The Country Gentleman* described the evolution of her modern kitchen.

Laura's woodstove in the Rocky Ridge house *(left)*.

Almanzo's gift to Laura in De Smet was this clock *(above)*. Until his death, he wound the clock each night.

Mary's nine-patch quilt, on exhibit in the museum at Rocky Ridge.

Laura's favorite rocking chair.

Laura, Almanzo and their dog Nero at the new house.

The Wilder plot, Mansfield Cemetery.

Rock house built by Rose for her parents as a retirement home. They lived there from 1928-1936, while Rose occupied the old farmhouse. The house still stands on a remote part of Rocky Ridge Farm.

Laura and Almanzo (*left*) during the "Summer of '42", photographed by "The Scribbler's Club" who visited from Topeka.

Laura, in the 1950's, was enjoying some of her honors (*above*) in the Rocky Ridge Library. One of the few natural color pictures of Mrs. Wilder.

Almanzo and brother Perley (*below*) riding in the ravine behind Rocky Ridge farmhouse.

The rock formation and cave (*below left*) in the ravine (with spring) behind the Wilder house.

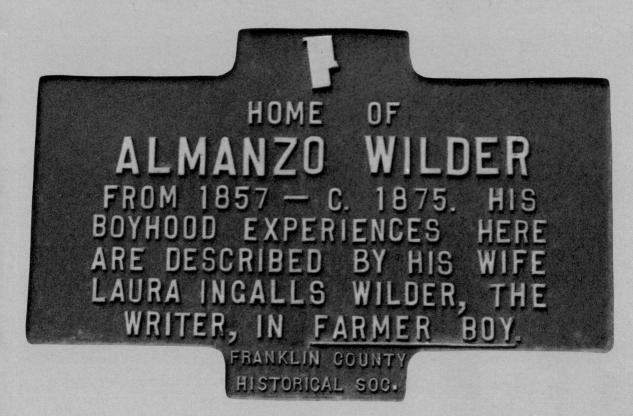

HOME OF
ALMANZO WILDER
FROM 1857 — C. 1875. HIS
BOYHOOD EXPERIENCES HERE
ARE DESCRIBED BY HIS WIFE
LAURA INGALLS WILDER, THE
WRITER, IN FARMER BOY.
FRANKLIN COUNTY
HISTORICAL SOC.

Site of *Farmer Boy* (above) near Malone, New York. The original Wilder farmhouse is presently being restored.

Carrie Ingalls' years in Keystone, South Dakota are remembered by the Keystone Historical Society. Her home was within two miles of Mount Rushmore.

Rose Wilder Lane in the bay window of her Danbury, Connecticut home in the 1960's. She died there in 1968.

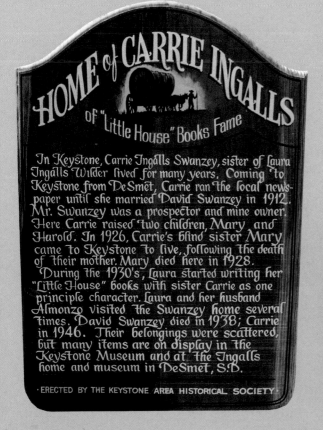

HOME of CARRIE INGALLS
of "Little House" Books Fame

In Keystone, Carrie Ingalls Swanzey, sister of Laura Ingalls Wilder lived for many years. Coming to Keystone from De Smet, Carrie ran the local newspaper until she married David Swanzey in 1912. Mr. Swanzey was a prospector and mine owner. Here Carrie raised two children, Mary and Harold. In 1926, Carrie's blind sister Mary came to Keystone to live, following the death of their mother. Mary died here in 1928.

During the 1930's, Laura started writing her "Little House" books with sister Carrie as one principle character. Laura and her husband Almanzo visited the Swanzey home several times. David Swanzey died in 1938; Carrie in 1946. Their belongings were scattered, but many items are on display in the Keystone Museum and at the Ingalls home and museum in DeSmet, S.D.

· ERECTED BY THE KEYSTONE AREA HISTORICAL SOCIETY ·

Painted on tin *(above)* by Laura Ingalls Wilder in the 1880's. Three of these primitive art pieces are on exhibit at the Laura Ingalls Wilder Home in Mansfield *(see back cover)*.

Laura's childhood paintings on tin were to illustrate trees for her sister Grace, who only remembered the prairie.

Helen Sewell drawing from original edition of *Farmer Boy.*

The timeless appeal of the "Little House" books constantly wins new readers for Laura Ingalls Wilder.